A Question of Perspective.

Insights from a Crime Writing Mystic.

Peter Mulraney

Copyright © 2016 Peter Mulraney

All rights reserved. No part of this book may be reproduced in any form or by any electronic or mechanical means, including information storage and retrieval systems, without written permission from the author, except for the use of brief quotations in a book review.

ISBN-13: 978-0-6482661-6-7

This edition published 2019.

To fellow pilgrims on the journey of life.

CONTENTS

Introduction	1
Superman	3
Graveyards	6
Edict from a self appointed authority	9
Transitions	12
Through the mind's window	15
Teachable moments	18
What story are you telling?	21
On being a mystic	24
Dying days	26
Who do you think you are?	29
The myth of time management	32
4 Types of commentators	34
The other story	36
The essential rule for staying in control	38
Creating a meaningful to do list	40

Happiness	42
A question of perspective	44
Prosperity	45
Harmony	48
Generosity	50
Collaboration	52
Keeping a journal	55
Who? Me?	58
The secret of appreciation	61
A note from Peter	65
Illustration credits	67
Also by Peter Mulraney	68

INTRODUCTION

A Question of Perspective is a curated collection of articles from my blog designed to give you an idea of what I mean by insights.

I'm a long time student of mind-body-spirit or metaphysical writers, which is how I got onto this mystical path. Some people call this material New Age but, when you look into it, it's actually only a modern expression of the perennial wisdom that sparked most of what people regard as sacred scriptures.

The challenge being presented to us today by spiritual writers is to question what we have been told to believe by our cultures and religions. This is the journey of the mystic, which is not an easy one in a world that emphasises the external and runs from examining the internal, where the answers that will set you free are to be found.

It's difficult because you need to firstly become aware of the beliefs and assumptions underpinning your behaviours and, then, decide what you choose to believe, and act accordingly.

The mystical path is about taking back your power from others. Some people won't like it when you do, but it's the only way to freedom.

I invite you to come on the journey, and recommend two practices if you are interested in joining me: meditation and journal writing.

There are many forms of meditation, and I've tried a few. My current practice is mindfulness meditation but there is nothing wrong with contemplative prayer or Transcendental Meditation - or any meditative practice that allows you to become aware of what you're thinking. The best part of meditation is the practice of taking the time to stop and intentionally spend some time with yourself. I call this the gift of silence.

Journal writing allows you to record your inner discoveries. One practice worth trying is free writing, where you ask a question and then simply write whatever comes to you without being critical of it as you write. It's a great a way of uncovering deeply held thoughts and beliefs.

I've included an article on keeping a journal, which mentions that I have designed a couple of *Sharing the Journey Coloring Journals* to help you get started.

You can read a larger collection of articles from my blog in *Sharing the Journey: Reflections of a Reluctant Mystic*.

Peter Mulraney, May 2016.

SUPERMAN

What is it about Superman we find so attractive?

I don't know about you, but I like the idea of flying without having to make a reservation, go through customs and border protection, or worry about the flight being cancelled, hijacked or worse.

I'm not so keen on the fancy costume with the underpants on the outside and the flapping cape.

I guess we would all like to be invincible. Or is that invulnerable?

Did you notice that the creators of Superman couldn't quite bring themselves to make him totally invincible? They gave him a weak spot. Interesting that they chose a piece of his home planet as the weapon that could undo him.

A bit like being vulnerable to home truths - those little things that only those closest to us know, which can be used to pull the rug out from under us when we go that little bit too far in public. Isn't it interesting that those who love us the most are the ones who take the wind out of our sails the quickest?

Who was the one person that could get Superman to do anything? Yes, you got it; Lois Lane. So they didn't make him invulnerable either.

Not so sure I would want to be rushing about the place saving every damsel in distress or chasing down every criminal wreaking havoc on society. I mean, why would you want to let everybody else off the hook of taking responsibility for their actions? No. I've resigned from being the general manager of the universe, and that includes being the saviour of the world.

Superman would certainly be busy if he was around today, what with all that stuff going on in Syria and Iraq, and who knows how many other places. I wonder if the man of steel could withstand a rocket-propelled anti-tank round the way he can withstand a speeding bullet. Come to think of it, tanks are made of steel, so maybe not. It seems even superheroes have limitations, and I guess back in the 1930s no-one imagined the sort of troubles or weapons we would bring into existence in the early twenty first century.

There's one thing about Superman though that I think we are all emulating. We're all hiding behind a version of mild-mannered reporter Clark Kent. We're keeping our real strengths and talents hidden, mainly because we don't trust ourselves or believe in ourselves enough to live authentically. Some of us are so much into being Clark Kent we aren't even aware of our Superman nature.

It's only when you've travelled some distance on the inner journey that you realise there is a lot more to your nature than you were led to believe. But you won't discover what that nature is unless you're prepared to look under the mask and find out who really is in there, and nobody can tell you who you'll find. You need to discover that for yourself.

You wouldn't believe me anyway.

GRAVEYARDS

I was in a graveyard or cemetery the other week attending a funeral.

According to Wikipedia, cemetery means sleeping place. How's that for optimism?

On the way home from that funeral, my son asked me how many funerals I'd attended over the years.

I've been to three in the last twelve months, but I started going to funerals as an altar boy, more than fifty years ago. It was one way of skipping half a day of school. So the first funerals I attended were for people I didn't really know. I might have known the person's name, but let's be honest - ten year old boys don't know that many old people.

The first family funeral I remember attending was my grandmother's. I was thirteen. I went with my father. In fact, we had driven all day to get to the hospital before it was too late. She died twenty minutes after we arrived at her bedside. It was as if she had held on until her favourite son arrived. That ended up being a week away from home - a holiday with my cousins. Don't recall why my father took me and not any of my brothers. Can't ask him now, because I've been to his funeral as well.

To be honest, I've been to so many funerals over the last forty or fifty years that I have lost count. Some have been harder to attend than others. I think one of the more difficult was that of my name-sake cousin. I can tell you, it's a strange feeling standing next to a casket with your name on it.

I've witnessed a range of emotions on display at the graveside - from stoic acceptance right up to hysterical wailing as the casket is lowered. It's just as well we are understanding of expressions of grief, even if we feel uncomfortable when someone totally loses it.

I've been to some good family wakes over the years. Something Irish families in the diaspora do pretty well. I've been to a lot of somber Italian funerals too - they seem to have a different take on death and dying.

On reflection, I've noticed something else. I don't visit graves. I go to the funeral but I never go back, unless we are slipping another casket into the same grave. As far as I'm concerned, it's over when I leave the cemetery.

Why do some people visit the grave every week? Why do some spend a fortune on tombstones?

If you wander around a cemetery and look at tombstones, it's like there is a competition to see who can erect the biggest memorial. Personally, I think there are better things you can do with the money.

From my perspective, cemeteries are places we use to dispose of bodies that are no longer required. We are returning the components to the earth. For the process to be completely natural, you'd think we'd bury bodies in caskets that break down easily once in the ground, or rely on cremation and simply scatter or bury the ashes.

I've been to funerals where the body was buried in a stainless steel, fibreglass covered, vacuum sealed casket in a cement lined grave. How quickly do you think a body buried like that would be reabsorbed back into the natural cycle? And we thought the Egyptians were crazy with their pyramids and mummies.

It's all a matter of perspective. What's yours?

EDICT FROM A SELF APPOINTED AUTHORITY

Friends, we live in interesting times.

A self-styled authority, operating within a self-proclaimed state, has issued a command to his followers and sympathisers around the world to commit random acts of violence in the name of his cause.

Nothing new there, you say.

The message might not be new - it's as old as the notion of empire itself - but the means of its delivery was via modern high-tech cyberspace, giving it an instantaneous worldwide audience, which our media outlets were only too willing to enhance.

Disturbingly, we have since witnessed deadly acts of violence in response to this call.

The powers that be on the world stage are responding in their chosen fashion as well - more violence, just a different type.

As a self-appointed authority of love, I've decided on a different response. I've decided to issue an edict authorising random acts of love and kindness.

Peter's edict to commit random acts of love and kindness

Friends, in the name of love, I authorise you to commit random acts of love and kindness on members of the public in the nation where you live, regardless of race, religion, age or occupation.

See the people in front of you, wherever you are.

Smile and greet each other.

Be welcoming to all in your community, especially those that appear different to you.

It doesn't matter what they are wearing.

Each person you meet is a brother or sister.

Talk to each other.

Listen to each other.

Find what you have in common and learn from your differences.

Share what you have to give and receive what others have to give to you.

Care for each other.

Help each other.

Speak kindly of each other.

The choice is always between love or fear.

Choose love every time!

Remember, we are all in this together, so share this edict with your friends, and let love be expressed across the face of the earth.

Peter's Edict

Commit random acts of love and Kindness!

TRANSITIONS

Life is full of transitions. We are always moving from one thing to another or morphing from one state of being or doing to another.

Every morning we transition from sleeping to waking, only to reverse it all again at night - and wouldn't you love to know where you go when you're sleeping? It all seems so vague to me after the morning transition back to wakefulness.

It's not only the things around us that are changing. We seem to be changing as well. At least as far as form or appearance goes. The reflection I see in the mirror these days only bears a faint resemblance to the images captured on 35 mm film when I was a younger man, when digital photography was still hidden in some dream state. Ageing is another expression of transition, although, thankfully, it's a slow motion experience for most of us.

Once, when we were warriors, we had initiation rites for significant transitions. Now we're expected to just get on with it. The end result, in our modern world, is we tend to skate on the surface of life and ignore the deeper issues. We experience our transitions as anxieties and treat them with pills, instead of immersing ourselves into them as opportunities for personal growth.

Some transitions can be painful, like the one going from being married to being divorced - and not only for the couple but for all those around them. That's one transition that a lot of us do not do well, because we don't know how to let go in a loving way or we refuse to allow the other to grow when we want to stay the same or vice versa. Another painful transition for some is moving through adolescence to young adulthood - and that one can be painful for all those around certain parties as well, and it's not always the kids causing the pain.

Sometimes, when you're in transition, you're aware that you're leaving one way of being but you're not quite aware of where you're going or how you're going to get there or what it's going to be like when you do get there, wherever there is. I'm entering into one of those transitions now.

After forty years in the workforce, retirement is looming on the horizon and, in my part of the world, the very nature of retirement itself is changing. Once you got a gold watch, played a few rounds of golf, went on a trip and then died. Now, thanks to modern medicine, electricity, food abundance and retirement savings plans, some of us can look forward to twenty or thirty years or more of post workforce life.

For many of us, the idea of retirement is scary. If you have your identity wrapped up in what you do, you wonder who you will be when you stop doing it. If you're in charge of a work team or a workplace, you wonder who you will be when you're no longer in charge of anyone or anything. If your life is your work, you wonder what will be your life when the work part is gone.

This is one of those transitions you need to put some serious planning into, otherwise you risk waking up one morning with nothing to do, no-one to play with and sixteen hours to kill before you can transition back to sleeping.

Retirement requires a plan.

THROUGH THE MIND'S WINDOW

When you enjoy a vista through a window, it feels like you are looking out onto the world.

Is that, in fact, possible, let alone true?

Science tells us that, in reality, you allow energy, in the form of light, to stream in through your eyes into your brain, and then you interpret the signal in your mind.

You are seeing with the mind's eye, and not with those two windows allowing the light into the mind.

What you see is not what's actually there in front of you but what you interpret as being there.

All of us are interpreting those visual signals in accordance with our unique perspective, constructed from our life experiences and our beliefs about the world.

Any two of us can look upon a scene and see it very differently, depending on who we are and what experiences we have had. In other words, we only see our opinion of what's there.

This is why the spiritual masters encourage us to pay attention to how we see things. This is why they say what we see is illusion.

If you want to see clearly, you need to become aware of the many filters in use in your mind. These filters are the beliefs that color your interpretation of the visual signals received in your brain. We call these filters prejudices, because they predispose you to certain interpretations. You can only remove a filter if you are aware of its existence.

For example, we all come into the world blind to color and race. Just look at how little kids behave in multi-racial settings. But how many of us lose our blindness to color and race by the time we are adults?

You can only regain that blindness by becoming aware of your color and racial filters, and then discarding them. You need to pay attention to the way you behave, and become aware of the thoughts you entertain, when you encounter people different to your social, racial or religious group if you are to regain that blindness you were born with.

One process for doing that is mindfulness, which involves slowing down and noticing what's going on inside your mind before you act - or say something you could regret.

As we become more aware of the way our minds work, it's up to us to exercise control of our minds, instead of relying on our past experiences and beliefs to interpret the world for us.

TEACHABLE MOMENTS

Life is a series of moments.

Every one of those moments is a teachable moment.

Sometimes it feels like you are being asked to take the role of teacher.

At other times you know you are the student.

Eventually, you realise that no matter what role you think you are playing, you are always Life's student.

It's easy to miss Life's teachable moments, unless you are paying attention to what's going on around and within you.

If you are always plugged into your device, playing games, reading Facebook or Twitter feeds, listening to music or podcasts, or texting some absent friend; how aware are you of what's going on around you? Can you even notice what's going on inside you?

Yes, you can access a lot of information through your smartphone or tablet while you are riding public transport or filling in all those empty spots in your calendar. If we're honest though, most of it is noise.

Sometimes, I wonder whether we are plugged into our devices because we are afraid of Life. We're busy avoiding her teachable moments, because we fear she might ask us to confront something that will burst our cosy reality bubble.

It's one thing to be concerned about the conflict in some far away country. It's something altogether different to deal with conflict in your immediate environment, and absolutely terrifying to have to deal with it in your relationship with your significant other.

The conflict in that far away country is not a teaching moment for most of us. The teaching moment is there where you are, and there in your relationship. The conflicts we see on the news are reflections of the conflicts in our lives that we refuse to address.

Those moments of conflict in your life become teachable moments when you engage with the one in front of you, and embrace the moment.

If there is one thing I've learnt on this journey it's that Life is a patient teacher - she keeps presenting you with teachable moments until you notice and engage with the lesson. So do yourself a favour and get your head out of cyberspace every now and then, and check in on what's really going on in your life.

It's much better to hear Life's teaching prompts when they're a whisper.

She'll knock you for six if she has to shout to get your attention.

WHAT STORY ARE YOU TELLING?

Every moment of every day is story time.

Take a moment and listen to that voice in your head.

What story are you telling yourself about yourself today?

Whether you're aware of what you're doing or not, you are telling your story all the time. You're telling it in your self talk and when you're telling others about yourself. You're telling it in all those thoughts you have about yourself.

What story are you telling? Are you putting yourself down? Are you limiting your possibilities by saying that there are things you can't do? Qualities you can't have? Is your story the same as everybody else's?

Are you deliberately crafting your story or simply repeating the same story over and over?

Who is the author of the stories you tell yourself about yourself? Is it you?

You can be the author of your story but you need to make that a deliberate choice.

If you don't pay attention to your storytelling you end up repeating things - mindlessly. Those things could be lies. They might have been true once, but there is a fair chance they are nothing more than opinions - that you have not consciously examined.

Here's something to think about. If you keep telling the same story nothing changes. If you want things to change in your life you need to start telling a new story.

Start telling yourself the story of who you want to be - and grow into being that person.

You won't change when things around you change.

Things around you change when you change - and you need to tell yourself a new story if you want to change.

I know this sounds easy but, in reality, it's a real challenge - simply because we are creatures of habit. It's so easy going with the flow of the familiar. It takes commitment to make a deliberate choice to change the narrative of your story - and to stick with that choice.

You also have to contend with peer pressure - from those people who want you to stay the same.

The fun is in the changing, not in the staying with the herd. So, go for it.

ON BEING A MYSTIC

Once upon a time, I thought that being a mystic was all about prayer, fasting and meditation - and living in the spiritual realms of existence.

You know, being a living saint like, say, Francis of Assisi or a modern day holy man like Bede Griffiths.

No wonder I was a little reluctant to heed the call. I mean, who wants to live like that?

I was misinformed.

Sure, some mystics might pray, meditate and fast - but being a mystic is about being fully engaged in the life you're living here on planet earth - otherwise you wouldn't be here.

It's not about escaping to some cloud of unknowing or any other nirvana. No, it's about finding out who you are and why you're here - this time.

The challenge is to be present and aware - and that's how you become a mystic.

Meditation helps you become aware but you need to choose to be present.

It's amazing what you notice when you're aware of the filters in your mind and you choose to be in the present moment.

You won't know what it's like until you give it a go.

It's as easy as breathing.

DYING DAYS

They spent hours strolling along the beach in the *dying days* of summer.

What are dying days?

In the context of the sentence above, they are the dwindling days or the last days of summer. They represent that period of transition from the pleasant season of summer to the chill winds of autumn - announcing the imminent approach of winter coldness.

They're romantic sounding words, evoking images of warm evenings, gentle breezes, and a foreboding of things coming to an end. These are the summer days we do not want to end.

Dying days take on a more sinister tone within the context of a murder mystery, where we often find ourselves dealing with an examination of the days leading up to someone's untimely death. Now there's another interesting description - untimely death.

Death is, after all, a natural event but we generally only regard it as timely when it occurs naturally, that is without assistance from an outside force - like a blunt instrument being applied to the head.

I wonder what each of us would do differently if we knew we were living our dying days, that dwindling number of days leading up to our untimely death. In one sense, every day is a dying day of life - you don't want it to end and, once it's gone, it's gone forever. Like all those glorious days on the beach.

Isn't it intriguing how we live as if we will be here forever?

Yet, we all know that there will come a day when we aren't living our dying days but our dying day.

It's fascinating reading about someone else's untimely death within the context of a crime novel, and consoling to know that crimes can be solved and justice applied, but what is it that attracts us to this genre?

As a writer, it's about creating a web of intrigue based on the darker side of life, taking myself into places in words that I would never go in life. In the last week, for example, I have spent my nights plotting and then executing a triple murder - all without leaving the house or picking up a weapon.

I wonder why people do things like kill their partner. And, when you read real crime stories as opposed to crime fiction, you discover that people do terrible things for very trivial reasons.

Maybe we read crime novels because fictional crime is more exciting than the real stuff. It's definitely a lot safer.

WHO DO YOU THINK YOU ARE?

'*Who do you think you are?*' is a popular BBC TV genealogy program that has spread to other countries, including Australia, Canada, Ireland and the United States.

In Australia, its screening is sponsored by ancestory.com, where you can explore your own family history.

It seems we're all interested in finding out about the family histories of so called famous people, going by the popularity of the program.

The success of family history sites like ancestory.com suggests we're interested in our own family histories as well. The question is - why?

Do you believe who you are is determined by your position in your family tree?

If you know the stories of the families you belong to - does that actually tell you who you are?

Or does it merely give you the context into which you were born?

After all, you are not your grandfather - no matter what amazing things he did in his lifetime.

Maybe you've benefited from the material success of the people who make up your bloodline - maybe you haven't.

What difference does it make to know that your great-great-grandmother was a slave? Look back far enough, if the records exist, and we all have a slave or two in our genealogies - that was the lot of most people, in most parts of the world, at one time or another.

Rome might have been ruled by Caesar but it was built and operated by slaves.

Delving into your family history is entertaining, and it can reveal glimpses of the lives people lived in previous eras. We can all learn something about the story of life on earth from such research. If you have the time, the inclination and the cash, go ahead and have fun.

While you're enjoying yourself, keep in mind that you are no more defined by your genealogy than you are by your nationality - they are both just stories.

You can choose to believe that you are defined by other people's stories - your choice - but why limit yourself.

THE MYTH OF TIME MANAGEMENT

Do you believe in time management?

Going by the number of books published on the topic it looks like a lot of people do.

I don't know what makes anyone think they can manage time.

Time is a concept.

It's flows like a stream but, unlike water, it cannot be contained.

We fool ourselves thinking we have it locked inside clocks or planners.

We measure it.

We schedule it.

It keeps going even when we aren't looking.

We all have the same amount of it available to us every day but some of us seem to do a lot more with our daily allocation.

Some of us make use of daily planners, scheduling our use of time - and this is where all those theories of time management come from.

I don't know about you but I have noticed that simply using a daily planner to schedule appointments and tasks does not necessarily mean those things get done as planned, despite the best of intentions.

In the final analysis, it's not time that has to be managed - it's our use of time, and that comes down to something which distinguishes the successful from the others: self-discipline.

If you ever read *The 7 Habits of Highly Effective People* by Stephen Covey, you'll discover he discusses time management under habit 3: Put first things first - principles of personal management.

I reckon he was onto something.

4 TYPES OF COMMENTATORS

I've been around for a while.

I've read a lot of commentary, listened to a lot of 'experts' on the radio, and watched a lot of interviews on TV.

I've come to the conclusion that there are four types of commentators.

The informed.

These guys have done their research. They've checked their facts and they know their subject. These guys are the subject matter experts.

The uninformed.

These guys think they know what they're talking about but they don't. They don't do any research, they make stuff up that sounds plausible. These guys are the bullshit artists.

The misinformed.

These guys have done some research but, sadly, they've mistaken the uninformed for the informed. These guys are the gullible parrots.

The intentionally misleading.

These guys have done their research. They've checked their facts but they have an agenda that does not include converting any of us into the informed. Their agenda is propagating misinformation.

These guys are the spin doctors.

So, be warned. You need to deploy your own bullshit detector, and question what every 'expert' tells you - including me.

Commentator alert.

Bullshit detector required.

THE OTHER STORY

During October 2015, I watched and listened to the presentations provided by the Mindfulness Summit. It was well worth the time investment.

One presentation was by Tara Brach. One story she told caught my attention, not for the actual content of the story but the message it held.

I've touched on the topic of the stories we tell ourselves before, but within the context of the stories we tell ourselves about ourselves.

Tara reminded me that we tell stories to ourselves about others.

Mindfulness is one way of becoming aware that we are listening to our stories about people, and not seeing the people in our lives.

If you're not quite sure what I mean, think of the labels you use to describe others. Try a couple of good ones like Muslim or Infidel; Christian or Atheist; Republican or Democrat; Conservative or Liberal.

There is always a person underneath the label - a person just like you.

There is only one source and we all come from that source. Using different names for source does not change the nature of source or our relationship with it or each other.

Something to think about the next time you catch yourself labelling another.

THE ESSENTIAL RULE FOR STAYING IN CONTROL

Want to stay in control of your life?

There is one essential skill to master: not panicking - no matter what happens.

Why is that essential?

As soon as you panic, you lose all objectivity and become subject to your fears, and there is no way you can make the correct decision once that happens.

When you don't panic, your response aligns with: 'Houston, we have a problem.' Instead of with: 'We're screwed!'

Your choice.

CREATING A MEANINGFUL TO DO LIST

To do lists. We all create them. Which list does your to do list look like?

List A:

- ❤ Eat - look after the body
- ❤ Pray - stay connected to Source
- ❤ Love - reach out to others
- ❤ Work - complete mundane tasks

List B:

☞ Work - complete mundane tasks

☞ Work - complete mundane tasks

☞ Work - complete mundane tasks

☞ Work - complete mundane tasks

We are not here to just work!

HAPPINESS

Several years ago, my wife bought a series of cards with Chinese characters depicting various emotions. One of them is the character for happiness.

We have them mounted in a picture frame on the wall of our family room.

I was looking at the happiness character the other night, from half way across the room, while I was eating, wondering how that pictograph conveyed the meaning of happiness.

I guess it would help if I had an understanding of Chinese characters but, in the absence of any such appreciation, I was taken by the picture of 'a man peering into a garbage can' - it reminded me of one of those guys you see fossicking for recyclables in any city.

That sort of gave me a jolt.

Is the picture telling us that happiness has nothing to do with circumstances?

Maybe the ancient Chinese were on to something.

A QUESTION OF PERSPECTIVE

One night, not so long ago, I listened to a visiting eminent American scientist being interviewed on Australian television. He was in the country to attend some exciting science symposium. As I listened to him talking about the nature of science, it occurred to me that there is a fundamental difference in the perspectives of science and spirituality.

Science is about exploring and gaining an understanding of the external world. Scientists are looking at the natural world - trying to figure out how it works and understand our place it in.

Spirituality is about exploring and gaining an understanding of the inner world. Mystics are looking within - trying to figure out who they are and how they are connected to the source of all being.

The problems come when practitioners write down their findings - and others insist that what is written is the truth.

PROSPERITY

We all want prosperity.

When we say that, what exactly is it we want?

Some starting pointers from the Oxford Dictionary:

- Prosperity/n. a state of being prosperous; wealth or success.
- Prosperous/adj. 1 successful; rich 2 flourishing; thriving 3 auspicious
- Prosper/v. 1 succeed; thrive 2 make successful.

Maybe it would be better to say we all want to prosper. We all want to succeed; we all want to thrive.

I suspect that most of us dream about the getting rich side of prospering.

There is nothing wrong with aspiring to be rich, but that's only one aspect of the state of being prosperous. Mind you, being rich enables you to do a lot more things than being poor, so it's understandable that we want to be richer than we are.

I think there is more to it than becoming rich.

What about flourishing as a person? What might that mean beyond or apart from having a healthy bank balance? What about healthy relationships? What about well-being and good health - physically, mentally and spiritually?

In a way, prosperity is about feeling good about yourself and being able to enjoy what this world has to offer.

If we think about prosperity as success, we can see that it's much more than just having a lot of money. Most of us know that's only one kind of success. We know that we can enjoy success in many aspects of life beyond accumulating money.

Maybe you can get that sense of prosperity simply by feeling happy with your lot. Maybe it comes from being in a loving relationship. Maybe it comes from living in communities where we respect each other or living in societies where everybody gets a fair go.

When you expand your definition of what prosperity means for you, as in the above examples, you start to see that there are no limits to prosperity. You start to understand that your prosperity adds to the prosperity of all and does not subtract from the prosperity of others.

If there is one thing I've learnt in life, it's you can't get what you want by focusing on what you don't want.

If you want to experience more prosperity in your life, decide what prosperity means for you, and devote your energy to creating more of that. That's what I'm doing.

HARMONY

Harmony has a range of meanings. The one I want to focus on is *the quality of forming a pleasing and consistent whole.*

Harmony in that sense has a meaning of working together for the benefit of all.

Each of us, I suspect, given the opportunity, would choose harmony over conflict.

I suspect we only choose conflict when we, as individuals or nations, act from self-interest in a competitive world.

When we act from the perspective of the common good, we are more likely to choose harmony.

In the world of sound, it's harmony that creates music and conflict that generates noise.

In the world of relationships, it's harmony that gives pleasure and conflict that delivers pain.

In the world of business, it's harmony that creates prosperity and conflict that generates exploitation.

In the world of international affairs, it's harmony that gives peace and conflict that delivers war.

I want to live in harmony with my lover.

I want to live in harmony with my family.

I want to live in harmony with my friends.

I want to live in harmony with my neighbours.

I want to live in harmony with the people that make up my nation.

I want to live in harmony with all people on earth.

Is that too much to ask?

GENEROSITY

Generosity recognises abundance - there is always more than enough to go around.

Generosity fuels an expanding universe - the more we give the more there is.

We can be generous with our love, with our awareness.

We can be generous with our nurturing, with our caring.

We can be generous with our time, with our attention.

We can be generous with our possessions, with our money.

We can be generous with our knowledge, with our skills.

We can be generous with our welcoming, with our inclusions.

We can be generous with our understanding, with our acceptance.

We can be generous as individuals, as families, as communities, and as nations.

Generosity knows that we are one, that we all belong to the one people populating the earth.

Generosity reminds us that we can't take any of earth's stuff with us when we leave the planet - not even our bodies. None of it belongs to us. All that stuff that pharaohs and emperors piled into their tombs is still on the planet, much of it redistributed by looters or archaeologists.

COLLABORATION

The act of working together to produce products or services.

Collaboration is the cornerstone of all successful societies and enterprises.

Before you question the veracity of that statement, think about how food ends up on your plate. Can you see the long line of people that collaborate to get it there? It starts with a farmer. It involves the person that made the plate and the person regulating the supply of gas or electricity to your kitchen. It ends with you. There are many others in the chain.

Even solitary pursuits, like writing a book, involve working with others to get that book into the hands of readers. Maybe you think that in today's world of self-published ebooks an author can do it all alone? It doesn't happen that way.

In my case, I'm collaborating with Amazon, who is collaborating with internet service providers, so that you can read books on your device of choice. Even Apple collaborates with Amazon so that you can download the Kindle App and read books purchased from Amazon on your iPad or iPhone. That's the thing with collaboration - all parties get something out of it.

Every employer - employee relationship is a collaboration. **Sadly, not all collaborations are based in equal relationships.** If they were, governments wouldn't be having discussions about increasing the minimum or basic wage and we wouldn't be hearing stories of exploitation of employees by employers.

Isn't it strange that we know that we need each other to be successful but, at the same time, we think it's okay or smart to take advantage of others in the name of self-interest?

Self-interest is the Achilles' heel of all societies and enterprises.

If you think that's a bit strong, what do you think is driving the regime in Syria? What do you think led to the 2008 global financial crisis? Why do you think the earth is polluted? Why do you think it's so challenging to get action on climate change? Why do you think we have special interest lobby groups?

I'd like to see more collaboration on working for the common good of everyone on the planet from every nation, community, corporation and individual.

It's not that hard. All it requires is that we recognise the short-sightedness of acting only in our own self-interest.

It's a small planet, friends; and we're all on it together breathing the same air.

KEEPING A JOURNAL

You unearth your patterns by reflecting on observations you record.

If you don't write things down your only record is memory; rightly regarded as an unreliable source of truth.

Keeping a journal is one way of creating a reliable written record for reflection.

Journals and journaling.

A journal can be a simple notebook or a purpose designed journal.

In a journal, you can create a record of the events that make up your daily life. You can record your reflections on those events, or on the greater questions of life that you'll ask when seeking meaning. If you meditate, you can record your insights. You can use your journal to problem solve or to record your dreams. If you like doodling, a journal is as good a place as any to store your doodles.

In today's digital age, keeping a hand written journal is one way of incorporating a practice that gives you both a break from your devices and a pause from your hectic schedule. It's a practice that encourages introspection, and allows you to read the story of your life in your own words.

A journal is a place where you can safely reinvent yourself and design the life you want to lead, while you're developing the courage to change your behaviours or beliefs. Like a caterpillar that goes into its chrysalis to work on its transformation into a butterfly, you can go into your journal to complete the work required to fuel your own transformation.

My journals.

As a long-time journal keeper, I recommend the practice.

I've designed a couple of journals you can buy from online bookstores to make a start or continue your practice.

WHO? ME?

When you're aware of your behaviour - you can do something about it.

It doesn't matter whether you're a criminal or a politician, if you have no awareness of how your behaviour impacts on your outcomes, you will continue blindly on your way to prison or losing your seat.

If you're in a relationship, continuing to ignore that your behaviour is impacting the quality of that relationship is an almost certain guarantee that relationship will fail - particularly if the other party is acutely aware of your behavioural imperfections. By the way, it doesn't matter whether the relationship is a romantic or a business partnership.

Self-absorption.

Most of us are self-absorbed, which I suspect is the default human position. Self-absorption allows you to look after your own interests, to push your own wheelbarrow regardless of the obstacles on your path. A little self-absorption is, no doubt, good for you. Total self-absorption is a recipe for disaster in a world based on relationships.

Slow down and observe yourself.

One way to become more self-aware is to slow down and pay attention to the way people respond to you.

Do people ignore you? Are they afraid of you? Do they resent your intrusions? These are not good signs if you notice them. On the other hand, if people welcome your participation, willingly work with you and want to be around you, it's probably a good idea to continue doing what you're doing.

It's also a good idea to reflect on what it is that you are doing that elicits whatever response you get from others. A little reflective downtime can help you identify behaviours that work, and others that may need some work.

Ask questions.

Another way to get an idea of how your behaviour impacts others is to ask them.

If you manage other people, you know how easy it is to be critical of their behavioural shortcomings. Well, guess what? Other people have been making their own assessments of your behaviour. Asking them how they see you is one way of finding out if you need to consider making a few changes. This one requires a little emotional maturity and a willingness to be vulnerable.

You might get a shock or a surprise. But, it won't kill you unless you choose to die of embarrassment.

In my opinion, it's better to risk a moment of embarrassment than to continue blindly on being an embarrassment to everybody around you.

Who? Me?

THE SECRET OF APPRECIATION

We are highly skilled at complaining about the things that are wrong in our lives. We all know what we don't want or don't have.

When was the last time you focused on the things that are working for you? The things that you have and want in your life.

The law of attraction.

According to the law of attraction, you attract into your life those things that you put your attention on. If you want more good things in your life, appreciating the good things already present is one sure way of attracting more of them.

The flip side of the law of attraction is that if you put your attention on the things that you don't want or don't have, you will continue to attract more of those.

For some reason, we tend to take the good things for granted and devote our energy to bitching about what we don't want or don't have. Now that you know about the law of attraction, you know what that means, don't you?

Actions to consider.

By giving up the bitching, you can refocus your energy on appreciating the things you have been taking for granted. In other words, stop complaining and put your attention on what is working for you in your current circumstances.

Look around you. The circumstances of your life reflect what you have been giving your attention to. Okay, it might not be all that pretty but, if you're reading this, somethings must be working for you.

Take a moment and identify the things, conditions, and relationships that support your wellbeing and prosperity. Acknowledge that you have attracted them into your life. Be grateful for them.

A few items that could be on your list of things to appreciate.

The people that love and support you: lovers, parents, friends, children, people that you work with.

People that serve you: shop assistants, postal workers, public transport drivers, police officers, teachers, government employees, farmers, truck drivers…

All those things that keep your body alive: air, water, food.

Things that provide bodily comfort: clothing, housing, electricity, plumbing, warm bedding in winter, air conditioning, microwave oven, gas cooktop, refrigerator, freezer, hot and cold running water, inside flush toilet, shower, washing machine, clothes dryer, windows, lighting….

The job or profession that provides your income. Even if you don't like your current job there is something about it that is working for you. Appreciate that part. That's the bit you want more of.

The secret.

The secret is to give your attention to the things you appreciate every day.

A NOTE FROM PETER

Hi, I'm a crime writing mystic from Adelaide, Australia.

If you enjoyed *A Question of Perspective*, please consider writing a review or sharing the book's details on social media to help other readers find the book.

In addition to the *A Question of Perspective*, I have several other books you might enjoy reading.

Sharing the Journey: Reflections of a Reluctant Mystic - explores the meaning of life and a few other interesting questions.

My Life is My Responsibility: Insights for Conscious Living - invites you to explore your beliefs and challenge your assumptions about life.

I Am Affirmations: The Power of Words and *Beyond the Words: Reflections on I Am Affirmations* introduce you to the power of affirmations.

Mystical Journey: A Handbook for Modern Mystics is a handbook for those ready to start the mystical journey - and for those who have set out on their own.

You can find details about all of my books and read my blog on www.petermulraney.com, where you can subscribe to my monthly newsletter 'Insights from a crime writing mystic'.

Or drop me a line at peter@petermulraney.com

Peter Mulraney

ILLUSTRATION CREDITS

Graveyards - Peter

Happiness - OpenClipArt.org

A question of perspective - Dmitrij Paskevic - Unsplash.com

Generosity - Alessandro Viaro - Unsplash.com

Collaboration - OpenClipArt.org

Keeping a journal - Sharing the Journey Coloring Journal cover

Who? Me? - Rafael H - Unsplash.com

Text illustrations generated with Art Text 3 from BeLight Software

Cover image - Luis Perdigao - Unsplash.com

ALSO BY PETER MULRANEY

Writings of the Mystic

Sharing the Journey: Reflections of a Reluctant Mystic.

My Life is My Responsibility: Insights for Conscious Living

I Am Affirmations: The Power of Words

Beyond the Words: Reflections on I Am Affirmations

Mystical Journey: A Handbook for Modern Mystics

Sharing the Journey Coloring Books

Mandalas

Mandalas by 3

Sharing the Journey Coloring Journals

Discovery

Reflection

Living Alone series

After She's Gone

Cooking 4 One

Sanity Savers

Living Alone (Collection)

Everyday Business Skills

Everyday Project Management

Everyday Productivity

Everyday Money Management

Novella

The New Girlfriend

Inspector West series

After

The Holiday

Holy Death

Whistleblower

Twisted Justice

The East Park Syndicate

Stella Bruno Investigates series

The Identity Thief

A Gun of Many Parts

Bones in the Forest

A Deadly Game of Hangman

Taken

Fallen